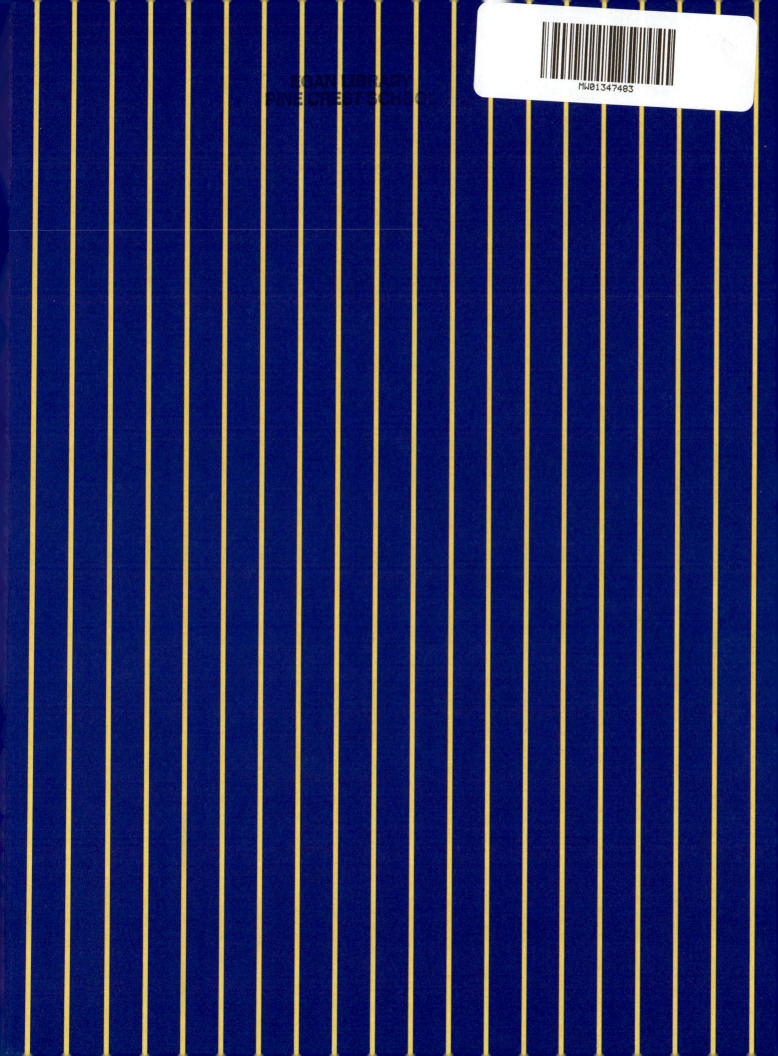

Bonnet House:
A Legacy of Artistry and Elegance

Bonnet House:
A Legacy of Artistry and Elegance

By
J. Kent Planck

Featuring Photography by
Bonnet House Fine Artists

J. Christopher Gernert
Annie Garrick
Sandy Dolan
and
Dan Routhier

Production Manager: Patrick Shavloske; Designer: S.MARK Graphics, Fort Lauderdale, Florida

All photographic copyrights credited by name. © Bonnet House, Inc. 2011. Fort Lauderdale, Florida. All rights reserved. No part of this book may be reproduced, stored in a retrieval system, or transmitted in any form or by any means, electronic, mechanical, photocopying, recording, scanning, or otherwise, without prior written permission from the copyright holder except for the inclusion of brief quotations in a review.

ISBN-13: 9780-9624-7575-7

ISBN 10: 0-9624757-5-0

For additional copies contact:
Bonnet House Museum & Gardens
(954) 563-5393
http://www.bonnethouse.org

Published 2011. First Edition.
Printed in the United States of America

Contents

Introduction
Page 5

The Land:
From Before History to Today
Page 9

The House and Its Decoration
Page 17

Utility and Whimsy
Page 27

The Collections
Page 33

How It Came to Be
Page 45

Timeline
Page 58

The "Jewel in the Crown"
Page 61

Epilogue
Page 75

Bartlett/Birch/Fortune
Family Tree
Page 80

Credits
Page 82

INTRODUCTION

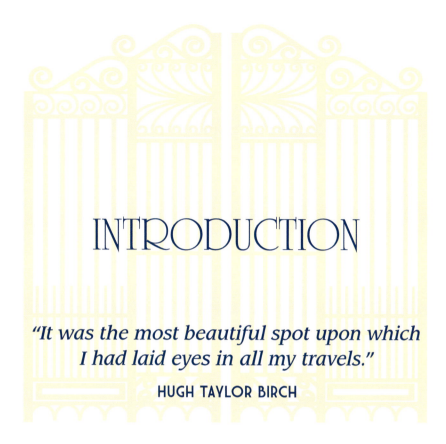

"It was the most beautiful spot upon which I had laid eyes in all my travels."

HUGH TAYLOR BIRCH

Bonnet House is an enchanting, eclectic oceanfront estate that epitomizes the lives and loves of those who created it.

In the early 1890s, Hugh Taylor Birch – a Chicago attorney and real estate investor – began purchasing hundreds of acres of South Florida oceanfront dunes. His daughter, Helen, would soon visit there with him and write starkly dramatic poetry to portray the exotic tropical landscape.

Twenty-five years later, Birch gave a two-thirds interest in much of that land to Helen and her new husband, Frederic Clay Bartlett. A noted Chicago artist, Bartlett was a young widower whose first wife, Dora Tripp, had also been trained as an artist and who had collaborated on some of Frederic's early work and shared his love of collecting. Now inspired by his new wife's reverence for nature and his own love of architecture and the decorative arts, Frederic fashioned an artistic winter retreat that survives today on 35 acres of Mr. Birch's original land.

Sadly, Helen was soon also lost to death, but Frederic remarried once more, to Evelyn Fortune Lilly, of prominent Indianapolis roots. Through her own painting, collecting, and gardening, Evelyn helped to vault the unique artistry of Bonnet House to even greater heights. Then, for more than 40 years after Frederic's death in 1953, she treasured and nurtured the estate's uniqueness: a mixture of architectural styles enhanced by unusual and rare collections and exotic plantings integrated with the natural tropical landscape. In 1983, fourteen years before her own death in 1997, Evelyn deeded the estate to the Florida Trust for Historic Preservation to protect for future generations what the Bartletts and Birches had created.

But what these families probably never fully understood – indeed, what we are only now coming fully to understand – is that so many others had previously walked and been inspired by this land: from prehistoric peoples who camped here millennia ago to northern Europeans who may have preceded even the Spanish as the first non-native peoples to explore it.

What we today call Bonnet House Museum & Gardens thus comprises one of the most unusual, eclectic, and historic house-museum sites in the nation. We are listed on the National Register of Historic Places and are accredited by the American Association of Museums. And we are dedicated not only to historic and environmental preservation but also to learning and creative expression, much like the Bartletts and Birches themselves. On this 90th anniversary of its creation, we are pleased to share with you both the treasures of this remarkable estate and the lives of those who created it.

Karen Beard
Chief Executive Officer
Bonnet House Museum & Gardens

(above) Frederic Clay Bartlett

(opposite) Evelyn Bartlett

THE LAND:
FROM BEFORE HISTORY TO TODAY

"Somehow it is the will of God for a man to work in the earth. The Bible tells us that the Lord God put man into the world to dress it and keep it. And that's what I like to do to help make the world more beautiful."

HUGH TAYLOR BIRCH

Archeologists have found evidence of Florida's earliest aboriginal people living here. Called *Tequestas* by Spanish explorers, they left behind an ancient midden of shell artifacts.

Although the Spanish also camped on this land, conch shells opened with knife blades suggest they were not the first Europeans to do so. Carbon-dated to the early 1500s, these shells point to earlier English or Dutch explorers who cut the shells to extract the meat instead of breaking off the ends as the Spanish would have learned from their earlier contacts with Caribbeans.

When Hugh Taylor Birch first saw the land in the 1890s, it was largely barren dunes, a narrow swamp cutting north to south through the center. This topography remains largely unchanged today. Spanning from the sands of the Atlantic beach to the mangroves along the Intracoastal Waterway, it continues to reflect the natural ecosystems of a barrier island.

Man-made alterations have been few and well-integrated: primarily, a canal – now lined with mangroves – dredged from the Intracoastal Waterway to bring building materials by boat and a freshwater lagoon dredged from the once-swampy depression between the dunes. The canal is now regularly visited by manatees, and the lagoon harbors native fish, turtles, and local and migrating waterfowl, as well as the yellow-blooming spatterdock lily, here nicknamed the "bonnet lily" after the name given the swamp –

Frederic Bartlett's desert garden has been replanted to look exactly as he created it in the 1930s.

Swans like those kept by Evelyn Bartlett grace the peaceful lagoon.

"Bonnet Slough" – on 19th- century maps. This lily, in turn, has since given Bonnet House its name.

Natural flora have been interspersed with ornamental and fruit-bearing plants: a Desert Garden of cactus and other drought-tolerant plants; paradise, mahogany, baobab, and kapok trees; royal palms along the lagoon; mango, avocado, star fruit, Rangpur lime, rose apple, and sapodilla trees, once joined also by pineapple, orange, and grapefruit. Thanks to Evelyn Bartlett's lifelong love of flowers, a thousand orchids flourish here. Hibiscus and bougainvillea flank the house, and gardenias and jatropha blaze in the courtyard.

A menagerie of animals calls Bonnet House home. In addition to the birds and marine life, grey foxes, gopher tortoise, monkeys, and even rare blue Atala butterflies thrive here along with the more-expected squirrels and raccoons. Evelyn Bartlett introduced black and white swans, demoiselle cranes, parrots, macaws, cockatoos, and pet monkeys, and Bonnet House still nurtures white swans, a caged green parrot, and a cockatoo. Squirrel monkeys roam the grounds, descendants of forebears once caged at a nearby bar who eventually found their way to the estate's lush landscape.

(above top) **Colorful spatterdock lilies are called bonnet lilies after the name *Bonnet Slough* given the swampy land on ancient maps.**

(above) **Conch shells found in an on-site midden show that both pre-historic peoples and early northern European explorers may have camped here.**

Bougainvillea, hibiscus, and other flowering plants brighten the tropical landscape.

(above) Springtime at Bonnet House occasionally sees the swan population temporarily expand.

(right) Squirrel monkeys continue to make the lush grounds their home.

Frederic Bartlett's design for a Caribbean plantation house included a central courtyard and a broad veranda but also incorporated vernacular and Moorish elements.

THE HOUSE AND ITS DECORATION

"The name Bonnet House...was chosen by Mr. Birch, who adored a little bonnet lily that grew along the marshland between the house and the ocean."

EVELYN BARTLETT

Though he was not trained as an architect, Frederic Bartlett personally drew the plans for Bonnet House in 1920.

Frederic eschewed the more formal Mediterranean Revival style then popular for South Florida estates and designed an informal Caribbean-style plantation house surrounding a central courtyard. But a tower with a graceful archway and large stone spheres atop looks decidedly Moorish. And the balconied, two-story eastern façade mimics the vernacular designs created by Edwin King, Fort Lauderdale's first building contractor, for the city's 1905 New River Inn and Mr. Birch's first Florida cottage. That Frederic intentionally borrowed and mixed architectural styles is not surprising. When he was a young artist in Chicago, one of his earliest mentors was architect Howard Van Doren Shaw who was known for doing the same.

A northerner used to the blustery winter shores of Lake Michigan, Frederic designed a house with outside stairways and no interior corridors in order to lead people outdoors in the mild Florida winters. Building materials were largely local or locally made: hollow cement wall blocks incorporating sand and manufactured on site; coral rock walkways; ceilings of cypress and Dade County pine. Rebar, still a young technology in 1920, was placed in the walls to protect against hurricanes. Surfaces were painted in bright primary colors.

In a characteristic flight of whimsy, Frederic Bartlett painted a *tromp l'oeil* faux marble balustrade across the studio loft.

Frederic purposefully did not design a fancy house or showplace for entertaining like so many grand houses of his day. He intended Bonnet House to be an informal family retreat. Its informality is reflected in the unique character of many of its rooms:

The Painting Studio, with its 20-foot ceiling, huge north-facing windows, marble fireplace, and storage loft, is reminiscent of French artist ateliers of the 1800s. Frederic's own special touch: a painted faux-marble balustrade across the front of the loft.

(right) Frederic Bartlett painted his new wife, Evelyn Fortune, in 1931, the year they were married.

(below) Frederic Bartlett's student portraits, on display in the studio, demonstrate his early artistic promise.

The Dining Room, used mainly for breakfasts, is octagonally shaped and houses a potpourri of collections: bright Portuguese tiles around a door, beer steins from Germany, mounted fish caught by Frederic and his son, Clay, and a wide variety of china.

The Drawing Room is a study in contrasts: the formality of a marble fireplace, leather wing chairs, and windowed alcoves against plain cement-block walls and a ceiling of rough-hewn wood. Frederic marbleized window frames and flanked the doors with ornate painted pillars from an antique church. Evelyn filled the room with images of animals – in statuary, on cushions, even on lamps.

(left) Frederic Bartlett framed a dining room door with colorful, hand-painted, antique tile from Portugal.

(below) The only paneled room in the house, the dining room displays a wide range of collections.

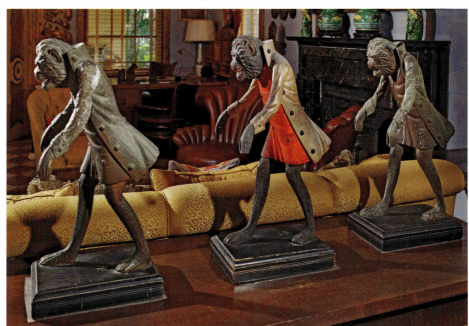

(above) The drawing room showcases oversized easel works by Frederic Bartlett, and his faux marble painting enhances door frames and other surfaces (above and page 16).

(right) Evelyn Bartlett's love of animals is reflected in her decorative taste.

(above) Created especially for Helen Birch, Bartlett's second wife, the music room features a classic Steinway piano and a bust for which even the lady's veil is carved from marble. (right)

The Music Room was originally designed for Frederic's second wife, Helen Birch, a composer and poet. The room contains a vintage Steinway piano signed by its namesake, two soaring, wall-mounted pier mirrors, and a magnificent marble bust of a veiled lady. The painted floor with center starburst was probably Frederic's last decorative creation finished one day prior to his suffering a disabling stroke in 1949 at age 76.

The Central Courtyard served as a "great room" for the Bartletts. With coral-rock walks, ornamental fountain, circus-like aviary, and lush tropical plantings, it provided a relaxing environment for family meals and entertaining. Covered perimeter walkways display carousel animals and colorful hand-carved Asian temple pieces exhibited on faux-painted marble-like table tops. On the walls: Frederic's primitive-style painted panels that were once a ceiling in a weekend retreat. Three high-ceilinged loggias received special Bartlett treatment. For one, Frederic trimmed borders and openings with local seashells; in another, he created a bright overhead mural of sea shells and marine life and then enlisted Evelyn to paint an intricate fishnet to unify it.

(right) **Carved animals, birds, and reptiles adorn antique, rosewood settees in the music room.**

(right) The butler's pantry displays Evelyn Bartlett's china and crystal against walls of blue copied from Ragdale, the Highland Park estate of Frederic's architectural mentor, Howard Van Doren Shaw.

(below) Frederic Bartlett's colorful courtyard aviary houses parrots like those kept by his third wife, Evelyn.

(opposite) A joint project of two artists, Frederic's ceiling mural of fish and seashells was unified by Evelyn's painting of a fishnet.

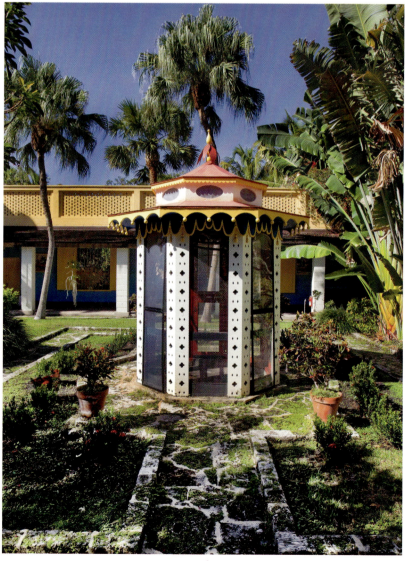

Many of the Bartletts' staff lived on site, with the caretaker and his family occupying this two-story cottage.

UTILITY AND WHIMSY

"To think that men could conceive such things, and actually bring them into being on a flat, bare canvas: Could create illusions of space, perspective, sunlight or storm, all on a piece of cloth with colors taken from dark mines or pungent earth, applied by means of bristles taken from a pig's back fastened to a little stick. All a glorious fake, of course, but how exciting."

FREDERIC CLAY BARTLETT, ABOUT PAINTINGS AT THE 1893 WORLD'S COLUMBIAN EXPOSITION

Several utilitarian structures flank the house: garages where the Bartletts' 1941 Cadillac convertible, one of only 400 manufactured, is on display, a caretaker's cottage, service structure, and boathouse. Rosie's Palace was once home to Mr. Birch's white mule. During construction, Rosie dragged building materials from the boat dock to the building site.

Frederic designed more whimsical structures to enhance the lighthearted and gracious Bartlett style.

The Bartletts entertained guests in an open-air pavilion at the south pond where Frederic hung bright canvases he had painted for Evelyn's 60th birthday party. They showed home movies in the South Seas-inspired Island Theater reached by footbridge in the center of the koi-filled north pond. Today, outdoor weddings are celebrated at a decorative dry fountain built of stone salvaged from a razed Palm Beach mansion.

Frederic's version of a thatched-roof, Seminole *chickee* bridges the lagoon and links the house to the Bartletts' beach path. The circular Shell Museum displays the Bartletts' vast collection of seashells and coral, and the adjacent Bamboo Bar once welcomed guests to enjoy the house drink – the Rangpur lime cocktail, a potent concoction of 150-proof dark rum, juice from the estate's unusual orange-colored limes, and Vermont maple syrup.

(above) The boat house gave the Bartletts easy access to the Intracoastal Waterway.

(right) The Bartletts' antique 1941 Cadillac convertible – one of only 400 manufactured – has won awards in local automobile shows.

(above) Tapestry-like paintings that Frederic created for Evelyn's 60th birthday party were later hung in this open-air pavilion.

(left) Frederic Bartlett might well be surprised that this dry fountain he constructed from stone salvage is now the site for weddings.

(below) The Bartletts' daily walk to the beach took them across Frederic's interpretation of a Seminole *chickee*.

(above) The Bartletts' shell and coral collection is displayed in the Shell Museum.

(left) Frederic Bartlett's design for the cozy Bamboo Bar was so precise that only two sticks of bamboo went unused.

(above) Evelyn Bartlett's orchid collection adds color and excitement to the Bonnet House décor.

(left) Frederic Bartlett's artist son, Clay, created this view of the Island Theater.

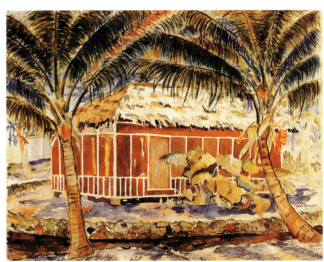

THE COLLECTIONS

"I am a collector...I cannot help buying curios, antiquities and works of art, even when I have no place to put them."

FREDERIC CLAY BARTLETT

Frederic and his first wife, Dora Tripp, built a mansion on Chicago's elite South Prairie Avenue. They called it *Dorfred House*, combining the first syllables of their names, and they decorated it with 19th-century artifacts, including religious pieces from travels in Germany and France. Many of these pieces are displayed in the Bonnet House painting studio.

Dorfred House

Frederic and second wife, Helen Birch, added blue-and-white Oriental pieces from their 1919 honeymoon to the Far East. They then spent much of their brief married life buying Post-Impressionist art in Europe, amassing a premier collection of work by Picasso, Toulouse Lautrec, Van Gogh, Cezanne and others – including, perhaps most notably, *(continued on page 39)*

Collections of European art and antiques filled Frederic and Dora Bartlett's Chicago mansion.

(above) *The Old Guitarist,* by Pablo Picasso, 1903

(right) *The Basket of Apples,* by Paul Cezanne, 1895

(below) *A Sunday Afternoon on the Island of La Grand Jatte,* by Georges-Pierre Seurat, 1884-86

The carousel menagerie has recently been restored to its original luster (also page 32).

Evelyn's courtyard collection of Asian palace and temple animals graces wooden tables designed by Frederic and surfaced with his signature faux marble painting.

Georges-Pierre Seurat's enormous pointillist work, *A Sunday Afternoon on the Island of La Grande Jatte*. The collection was given to the Art Institute of Chicago in Helen's memory following her 1925 death.

Though both Frederic and his third wife, Evelyn Fortune Lilly, were painters, they preferred to think of themselves as collectors.

Evelyn especially loved animals. Treasuring her pet dogs, birds, and monkeys, she displayed images of animals throughout the house – from Asian temple pieces in the courtyard, to monkey statuary and china lamps bearing intertwined snakes in the drawing room. Other collections include a wide variety of china and crystal, German beer steins, mounted fish caught by Frederic and his son, colorful carousel animals, sea shells and coral, a thousand or more orchids – even an array of simple colored glass bottles.

Perhaps most stunning of all is Frederic's and Evelyn's own artwork: Frederic's easel paintings in the studio and decorations throughout the house, and Evelyn's still lifes and portraits in the guest wing, now converted to a gallery.

Frederic Bartlett's paintings in the Bonnet House Courtyard exhibit a more primitive style and Frederic's appreciation of German folk culture.

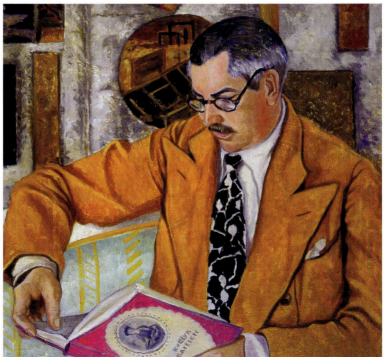

(above) Evelyn Bartlett painted her close friend, Catherine Eddy Beveridge, who was also Helen Birch's second cousin.

(right) Evelyn Bartlett painted a portrait of her husband, Frederic, entitled *Yellow Coat*.

(above and opposite) A guest once said you could eat at Bonnet House for a week and never see the same china twice.

(right) Where and how better than as an art student in Munich for Frederic to have amassed this collection of now-antique beer steins?

Frederic Bartlett's painting of the Bonnet House courtyard reflects the influence of the Post-Impressionists on his later work – in this case, of a courtyard painting by Paul Cezanne.

HOW IT CAME TO BE

"James McNeil Whistler arrived in Paris and opened a school...I was one of the first to enroll...The opportunity was too great to be missed."

FREDERIC CLAY BARTLETT

In October 1893, Hugh Taylor Birch, a prominent Chicago attorney, real estate investor, and naturalist, rode Henry Flagler's new Florida East Coast Railway south to its terminus at Titusville. There he borrowed a boat and sailed further south along the coast until a storm forced him into New River Sound at what is today Fort Lauderdale.

Wearied by the chaos of a burgeoning Chicago during the city's 1893 World's Columbian Exposition, Mr. Birch had come to seek land for a tropical retreat. Captivated by the raw beauty of the New River's desolate coastal landscape, Mr. Birch and a business partner, John MacGregor Adams, soon began buying inexpensive oceanfront land that would eventually stretch more than two miles along the beach.

The World's Columbian Exposition, Chicago, 1893

> *"He'll know my birds and
> my trees and my flowers
> And in friendship or in strife
> He'll be a man as I love a man
> And live a Good Man's life."*

HELEN BIRCH BARTLETT, FROM "BIG BOSS," A POEM WRITTEN AT AGE 15, ABOUT HER FATHER, HUGH TAYLOR BIRCH

Mr. Birch's daughter, Helen, wrote poetry, composed music, and shared her father's love of nature. By the turn of the century she was spending winters in Florida with Mr. Birch and capturing those experiences in poetry that reflected the exotic tropical environment.

Frederic Clay Bartlett, a neighbor and family friend of the Birches on Chicago's fashionable South side, had turned 19 in 1893. Frederic was captivated by the artistry at the Columbian Exposition and persuaded his father – wealthy businessman Adolphus Clay Bartlett – to allow him to forego a career at the family's prosperous wholesale hardware firm, Hibbard, Spencer, Bartlett & Company and instead study art.

Frederic studied with a private art tutor in Germany and was then accepted to the prestigious Royal Academy in Munich. There he fell in love with fellow student Dora Tripp from White Plains, New York. They were married in 1898 and went to Paris where Frederic studied with James Whistler and was inspired by the renowned muralist Pierre Puvis de Chavannes.

(above) Hugh Taylor Birch

(right) Shown at age 9, Frederic Clay Bartlett, Jr., who became a talented artist and musician, died two years after his father in 1955 at age 48.

(left) Dora Tripp Bartlett was once described as "one of the prettiest, sweetest, and most entertaining women" in Chicago's exclusive South Prairie Avenue neighborhood.

(below) Helen Louise Birch

After they returned to Chicago in 1900, Frederic prospered as an easel painter and creator of large, public murals. He painted in a 40-foot studio spanning the rear of their South Prairie Avenue mansion, and together he and Dora filled the house with antiques and artwork. Dora was a civic leader on social issues, and she and Frederic figured prominently in Chicago society. Winters were often spent abroad, summers at his father's Lake Geneva, Wisconsin, estate.

Only one of three children survived infancy – Frederic Clay Bartlett, Jr., born in 1907 and always called Clay. He was sickly much of his youth, and Dora struggled with neuralgia. In the fall of 1916, the family moved to New York, possibly to be closer to Dora's family, and Frederic was elected to the American Institute of Arts and Letters. But Clay developed pneumonia early in 1917, and after literally wearing herself out nursing him back to health, Dora died unexpectedly at the age of 37.

Disconsolate at his loss, Frederic later found comfort in the company of Dora's best friend Helen Birch, already a published composer.

"My first commission was to copy a daguerreotype of a handsome old gentleman. For this I received seventy-five dollars. I rushed across the street to the Art Institute where I had seen…a clever sketch…which I wished to purchase for my father."

FREDERIC CLAY BARTLETT

Frederic encouraged Helen to publish her poetry, too, and the couple soon fell in love. In January 1919, they were married at the home of Helen's cousin, Catherine Beveridge, in Beverly, Massachusetts, on Boston's north shore.

Hugh Taylor Birch gave the newlyweds a two-thirds interest in much of his South Florida oceanfront land. Inspired by Helen's love of nature and his own enthusiasm for design and decoration, Frederic drew plans for a winter retreat on what is today 35 acres of that land, and he and Mr. Birch supervised construction.

Driven by a joint love of art and the avant garde, Frederic and Helen spent much of their married life in Europe purchasing Post-Impressionist paintings.

Together with Mr. Birch, they purchased a more formal summer estate in Beverly. Frederic had it painted white and christened it *Whitehall*. After an extended trip through Europe and Egypt in early 1925, they returned there for the summer and had lunch one day with Evelyn Fortune Lilly, an Indianapolis friend of Helen's cousin Catherine and the wife of Eli Lilly, the grandson of the pharmaceutical founder. By late summer, Helen was diagnosed with cancer and died in New York that fall. She and Frederic had been married only six years.

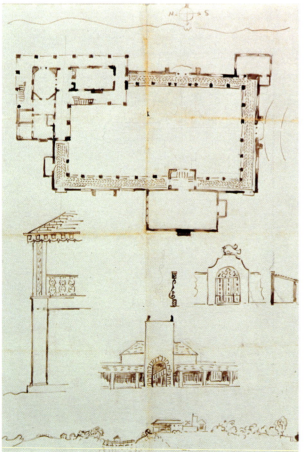

(above) Frederic Bartlett with his second wife, Helen Louise Birch.

(below) Bartlett sketched his original concept for Bonnet House on the back of a Bacardi rum label.

(left) Frederic Clay Bartlett, right, with (L-R) son Clay, Hugh Taylor Birch, Helen Birch.

(below) Rebar-reinforced cement blocks made on site using sand from the grounds created an informal but sturdy structure that has resisted hurricanes for decades.

Aerial photograph of Bonnet House, circa 1940.

Aerial photograph of Bonnet House today.

Following Helen's death, Frederic abandoned winters at Bonnet House to Mr. Birch and instead divided his time between Whitehall and an apartment in Chicago. In Beverly, he was consoled by his neighbor, Evelyn Lilly, now divorced after a difficult 19-year marriage. Frederic found himself consoling Evelyn, too, when her eight-year-old daughter, Evie, developed pneumonia. Over time, their relationship deepened, and in 1931 the two were married. Frederic was 58, Evelyn, 44.

Under the joint stewardship of the Bartletts and Mr. Birch, Bonnet House flourished in the 1930s and 40s. Frederic enhanced his decorative work and created other whimsical structures: an open-air pavilion, a dry fountain, the Island Theater and Shell Museum. The swamp in front of the house was dredged for a lagoon, and palms, fruit trees, and other specimens were added to the landscape. Inspired by her new artistic environment, Evelyn expanded a schoolgirl talent for drawing into an

"He was one of the kindest people I've ever known, great companion, great fun, handsome...everything perfectly delightful about him."
EVELYN BARTLETT, ABOUT HER HUSBAND FREDERIC

(below) Royal Palms, purchased with a birthday check from her father, were added by Evelyn Bartlett to the western shore of the lagoon around 1936.

exceptional five-year career as a self-taught still-life and portrait painter. Evelyn also purchased Bothways Farm in Essex, Massachusetts, where she could extend her gardening year-round and where Frederic designed additional whimsical creations. Together they continued to travel – mostly through Europe – and to collect art and artifacts.

Winters at Bonnet House were lived with style and grace, though little ostentation. Friends and acquaintances were many and often distinguished – from the art world, business, and politics – but guests were relatively few and usually only the closest friends. Bonnet House was a retreat; the Bartletts left a more hectic and elaborate social life behind up north.

The sizable Bonnet House staff was accorded the same respect and kindness shown to guests. Whether as caretaker, cook, butler, chauffeur, maid, laundress, or groundskeeper, staff members knew the Bartletts and Mr. Birch cared for them as people, not just employees. One said they treated each of them "like a member of the family," brought gifts from their travels, and even maintained homes for them on and off property.

In 1940, Hugh Taylor Birch built a new home for himself on land north of Bonnet House which he later gave to the state for the Hugh Taylor Birch State Park. Mr. Birch died there in 1943 at the age of 94. Six years later in 1949, Evelyn and Frederic's 22 years together began disintegrating when Frederic suffered a devastating stroke at age 76. His creativity and zest for life were shattered, and he died four years later at Whitehall, soon after his 80th birthday.

Several years before his death, Frederic and Evelyn had become fond of a retired stockbroker from

(above) Newlyweds Evelyn and Frederic Bartlett sailed to Europe in 1931.

Evelyn and Dan Huger continued the migratory Bartlett lifestyle, spending eight months of the year in Beverly and four at Bonnet House.

New York, Daniel Elliot Huger, the descendent of an illustrious South Carolina family. It's believed that Frederic suggested to Evelyn that when he died, she should marry Daniel – who was ten years younger than she – so she would have someone younger to look after her in her own old age. Soon after Frederic's death, Evelyn followed through on that wish, and together she and Daniel continued the annual migrations between Whitehall and Bonnet House and the gracious lifestyle at each. But contrary to what Frederic may have hoped, Evelyn was again widowed – this time, at age 80 – when Daniel died from cancer in 1967.

Evelyn never remarried. Instead, she concentrated on preserving what had been created by the Birches and the Bartletts. In 1983, she deeded the property to the Florida Trust for Historic Preservation. It was the largest charitable contribution that had ever been made in the state of Florida. Evelyn added only two stipulations: that she be allowed to spend winters here until her death, and that Bonnet House be preserved exactly as it had been when she and Frederic were here together in the 1930s and 40s.

Evelyn continued to spend winters here for another twelve years, until 1995, when the annual trip from Beverly simply became too arduous. In 1997, just three months short of her 110th birthday, she passed away quietly at Whitehall, secure in the knowledge that Frederic's and her beloved Bonnet House would be preserved forever just as they had known and treasured it.

Purchased in 1925, the Birch-Bartlett estate in Beverly, Massachusetts, was called *Treetops* until Frederic had it painted white and rechristened *Whitehall*. The house no longer exists.

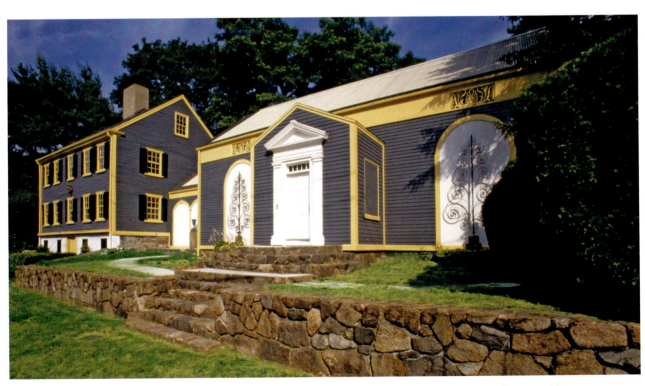

The art studio and gallery at Whitehall still stands, and it has been restored as a private residence.

Frederic Bartlett designed a tiered garden for a hillside at Whitehall.

Whitehall was a more formal estate than the Bartletts' South Florida retreat.

TIMELINE

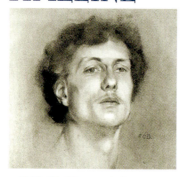

1893-95: Charcoal sketch by Frederic Bartlett.

1916: Frederic Bartlett creates *Blue Rafters* depicting his first wife, Dora Tripp, at their home in Lake Geneva, Wisconsin.

1920: Bonnet House construction begins.

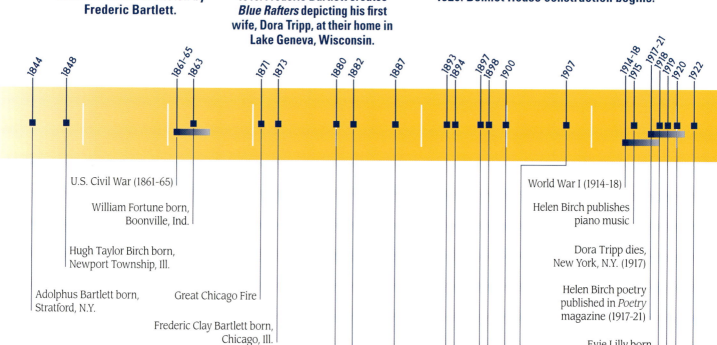

- **1844:** Adolphus Bartlett born, Stratford, N.Y.
- **1848:** Hugh Taylor Birch born, Newport Township, Ill.
- **1861-65:** U.S. Civil War (1861-65)
- **1863:** William Fortune born, Boonville, Ind.
- **1871:** Great Chicago Fire
- **1873:** Frederic Clay Bartlett born, Chicago, Ill.
- **1880:** Dora Squire Tripp born, White Plains, N.Y.
- **1882:** Helen Louise Birch born, Chicago, Ill.
- **1887:** Evelyn Fortune born, Indianapolis, Ind.
- **1893:** Hugh Taylor Birch makes first trip to Florida
- **1894:** Frederic Clay Bartlett to Royal Academy in Munich
- **1897:** Hugh Taylor Birch buys Florida land with John MacGregor Adams
- **1898:** Daniel Elliott Huger born, Nyack, N.Y.
- **1900:** Frederic Bartlett and Dora Tripp marry, White Plains, N.Y.
- **1907:** Frederic Bartlett launches painting career, Chicago, Ill.
- **1914-18:** World War I (1914-18)
- **1915:** Helen Birch publishes piano music
- **1917-21:** Dora Tripp dies, New York, N.Y. (1917); Helen Birch poetry published in *Poetry* magazine (1917-21)
- **1918:** Evie Lilly born, Indianapolis, Ind.
- **1919:** Frederic Bartlett and Helen Birch marry, Beverly, Mass.
- **1920:** Bonnet House construction begins; Adolphus Bartlett dies
- **1922:** Frederic Clay Bartlett, Jr. ("Clay") born, Chicago, Ill.; Evelyn Fortune and Eli Lilly marry, Indianapolis, Ind.

1938: Bothways Farm purchased.

1945: The Bartletts walk with friends to the main house.

1989: Evelyn Fortune Bartlett with her dog, Abbey.

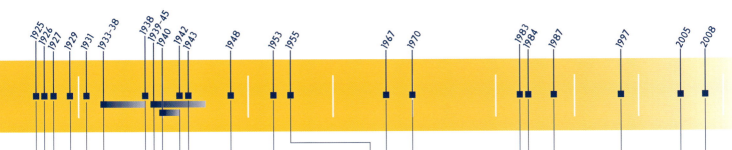

Timeline entries:

- 1925 — Helen Birch Bartlett dies, New York, N.Y.
- 1926 — Whitehall purchased, Beverly, Mass.
- 1927 — Evelyn Fortune and Eli Lilly divorce
- 1929 — Helen Birch Bartlett Collection given to Art Institute of Chicago
- 1931 — *Capricious Winds*, a book of Helen Birch Bartlett's poetry published
- 1933–38 — Hugh Taylor Birch donates Glen Helen in Yellow Springs, Ohio to Antioch College in his daughter's memory
- 1938 — Frederic Bartlett and Evelyn Fortune Lilly marry, Indianapolis, Ind.
- 1939–45 — World War II (1939-45)
- 1940 — Evelyn Bartlett paints (1933-38)
- 1940–42 — Nymphenglade built, Davie, Fla. (1940-42)
- 1942 — Evelyn Bartlett purchases Bothways Farm, Essex, Mass.
- 1943 — Hugh Taylor Birch deeds 180 acres of Fort Lauderdale land to the state of Florida for a park
- 1948 — William Fortune dies
- 1953 — Hugh Taylor Birch dies, Fort Lauderdale
- 1955 — Nymphenglade sold
- 1967 — Evelyn Bartlett marries Daniel Elliott Huger, Fort Lauderdale
- 1970 — Frederic Bartlett dies, Beverly, Mass.
- 1983 — Frederic Clay Bartlett, Jr. dies
- 1984 — Frederic Bartlett's student memoir, *Sortofa Kindofa Journal of My Own* published
- 1987 — Daniel Elliott Huger dies, Beverly, Mass.
- 1987 — Evie Lilly dies
- 1983 — Bonnet House listed on the National Register of Historic Places
- 1983 — Bonnet House deeded to the Florida Trust for Historic Preservation
- 1987 — Evelyn Bartlett celebrates 100th birthday
- 1997 — Evelyn Bartlett dies, Beverly, Mass.
- 2005 — Bonnet House grounds suffer significant damage from Hurricanes Katrina and Wilma
- 2008 — Bonnet House accredited by the American Association of Museums

Chicago architect Howard Van Doren Shaw commissioned the young Frederic Bartlett to create this *Tree of Life* mural for his restoration of the city's Second Presbyterian Church in 1900.

THE "JEWEL IN THE CROWN"

"This is truly a crown jewel. This estate will be far beyond a living museum. I think you'll find it'll be a major cultural center."

GEORGE FIRESTONE, FLORIDA SECRETARY OF STATE, 1979-1987

Though truly the "jewel in the crown" of all that the Bartletts and Birches created, Bonnet House is but part of the vast panorama of their creativity.

Leading American museums today own and display Frederic Bartlett's easel work – in Chicago, Detroit, Indianapolis, Philadelphia, and Washington, D.C. – and Frederic's most monumental mural work remains on view in his native Chicago: wall and ceiling decorations at the Second and Fourth Presbyterian Churches, and ceiling panels and stained glass at the University Club, a panoramic frieze at the University of Chicago depicting a medieval athletic tournament. His Chicago apartment – recently home to movie critic Gene Siskel, now deceased – still displays the modernist murals with which Frederic decorated the walls.

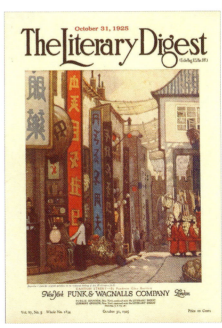

Frederic Bartlett's Chinese painting, *Canton Street*, was featured on the cover of the *Literary Digest* in 1925. The original painting is at the Corcoran Gallery in Washington, D.C.

In 1927, Frederic Bartlett painted jungle scenes on the music room walls at the Monticello, Illinois, estate of his life-long friend Robert Allerton.

Frederic Bartlett collaborated with Chicago architect Howard Van Doren Shaw on the design and decoration of House in the Woods, the Lake Geneva, Wisconsin, estate of Frederic's father.

(left) Frederic Bartlett's 51 painted panels of a *Gothic Chase and Feast* have adorned a ceiling at Chicago's University Club since 1909.

(below) Frederic Bartlett's 1908 designs for 14 stained glass windows at the University Club of Chicago were selected on the recommendation of Louis Comfort Tiffany over Tiffany's proposed designs.

(above top) In 1904, Frederic Bartlett created murals of Medieval games for the Frank Dickinson Bartlett Gymnasium at the University of Chicago, endowed by Frederic's father in honor of his brother who died in 1900 while a student at Harvard University.

(above) Frederic Bartlett painted this mural on the tenth floor of the Fine Arts Building in Chicago, Ill., the location of his art studio.

Frederic painted whimsical jungle scenes on the music room walls at the Monticello, Illinois, estate of Robert Allerton, his closest life-long friend, and he helped architect Howard Van Doren Shaw decorate the Lake Geneva estate, House in the Woods, that Shaw designed for Frederic's father.

Unfortunately, some of Frederic's work has been lost. Several of his Chicago murals have been covered up by building renovations or destroyed by fire, such as his 1913 work at the Chicago City Council chamber. Dorfred House is gone and with it his wall decorations there. Whitehall, too, has fallen victim to the wrecking ball, though the

(right) Frederic Bartlett's first wife, Dora Tripp, helped design the ceiling panels that Frederic created for Chicago's Fourth Presbyterian Church in 1914.

(below) At Bothways Farm, Frederic Bartlett decorated a children's playhouse with his paintings based on Currier & Ives lithographs, and christened the redecorated structure the *Picnic House*.

studio building remains as a private residence. The Picnic House at Bothways Farm – a former children's playhouse that Frederic lined with his painted reproductions of Currier and Ives prints – likewise has been destroyed, though the paintings now rest at Bonnet House.

More fortunate to survive is Frederic's Bothways Farm reproduction of a German hunting lodge, designed for parties after a rain shower at Evelyn's *al fresco* 60th birthday luncheon forced guests to seek shelter in the barn. Also surviving, though not restored: Nymphenglade, Frederic's miniature reflection of Munich's Nymphenberg Palace, built on the fringe of the Everglades as a weekend retreat.

All three of Frederic's wives are part of this broad creative heritage.

Germany's Nymphenberg Palace inspired Frederic Bartlett's creation of Nymphenglade, a weekend retreat near the edge of the Everglades.

Evelyn Bartlett purchased Bothways Farm in Essex, Massachusetts, still a working farm today.

Frederic Bartlett's Bavarian-style hunting lodge provided a whimsical site for entertaining guests at Bothways Farm.

CAPRICIOUS WINDS

BY
HELEN BIRCH BARTLETT

WITH A
BIOGRAPHICAL NOTE BY
JANET A. FAIRBANK

AND
AN APPRECIATION BY
HARRIET MONROE

Boston and New York
HOUGHTON MIFFLIN COMPANY
The Riverside Press Cambridge
1927

(above) More than seventy poems written by Helen Birch – many previously published in *Poetry* magazine – appeared in *Capricious Winds*, a book of Helen's poetry published posthumously in 1927.

(right) Both an accomplished pianist and composer, Helen Birch published several compositions written to accompany the words of prominent romantic poets.

Dora Tripp left a hand-written diary from the last four years of her life. It provides our only view of her and Frederic's days together – days of elegant international and cross-country travel, of Frederic's greatest public creativity, and of Dora's progressive social welfare leadership. And though we may not be able to identify Dora's specific contributions, Frederic's murals at Chicago's Fourth Presbyterian Church include her designs.

Helen Birch preserved in poetry the tropical mystery of the South Florida land from which the Bonnet House estate was later created. This and other poetry appeared in *Poetry* magazine in the late teens and early 1920s and in a posthumously published book, *Capricious Winds*. Helen also published musical compositions that she wrote to accompany the words of her favorite poets.

Evelyn Fortune left not only a significant body of paintings and extensive collections, but also a remarkable legacy of gracious living and hospitality.

> "[I] worked for Frederic on church designs in [the] Boat House . . . . Frederic and I worked all day on the panels for the dining room in the big house. We had a simple picnic luncheon at the studio."
>
> DORA TRIPP BARTLETT, FROM HER DIARY, REGARDING DESIGNS FOR MURALS AT CHICAGO'S FOURTH PRESBYTERIAN CHURCH, AND DECORATIONS FOR HOUSE IN THE WOODS, LAKE GENEVA, WISCONSIN.

Self-taught artist Evelyn Bartlett – whom Frederic considered to be one of his most delightful artistic discoveries – painted portraits and still-lifes that are now on display in the former guest wing.

"My father had always pointed out the good and bad features of buildings and houses since I was a very small boy... [H]e had also done much towards my [painting] education...and when he started his now well-known collection of Modern French Painters, I became extremely interested in those masters."

FREDERIC CLAY BARTLETT, JR., FROM "A PERSONAL HISTORY," 1942

Because of Evelyn's love of monkeys, Frederic purchased unusual monkey statuary at an antique shop in New York's Plaza Hotel. The statues had been created for the purpose of receiving calling cards of visitors.

Also part of the family's artistic legacy: Frederic Clay Bartlett, Jr., Frederic's son, was an accomplished artist, and Evelyn's daughter, Evie Lilly Lutz, produced ceramics.

The land itself looms large in this creative heritage, as does the man, Hugh Taylor Birch, who had the foresight to acquire it. Though much of his original South Florida land was sold for gain by those to whom he left it, Mr. Birch himself assured preservation of 180 acres through his gift of Birch Park, adjacent to Bonnet House, to the state of Florida. In Yellow Springs, Ohio, Mr. Birch bequeathed Glen Helen – 800 acres of pristine prairie, woods, and streams – to Antioch College in memory of his beloved daughter.

It's a remarkable heritage overall, and one that can only underscore – and not in any way detract from – the true jewel of that heritage that is Bonnet House Museum & Gardens.

Evelyn Bartlett made certain that dining at Bonnet House combined an elegant table setting with a delectable meal in a garden atmosphere.

Evelyn Bartlett's daughter, Evie Lilly Lutz, created plates, canisters, and a tureen for her mother and painted them with images of monkeys and coral.

*"The earth smells old and warm and mellow, and
all things lie at peace.
I too serenely lie here under the white-oak tree,
and know the splendid flight of hours all
blue and gay, sun-drenched and still."*

HELEN BIRCH BARTLETT, FROM THE POEM "UP IN THE HILLS," AS INSCRIBED ON A MEMORIAL TABLET AT GLEN HELEN IN YELLOW SPRINGS, OHIO.

Hugh Taylor Birch gave Antioch College 800 acres of woodlands in Yellow Springs, Ohio, that he named Glen Helen in memory of his beloved daughter.

EPILOGUE

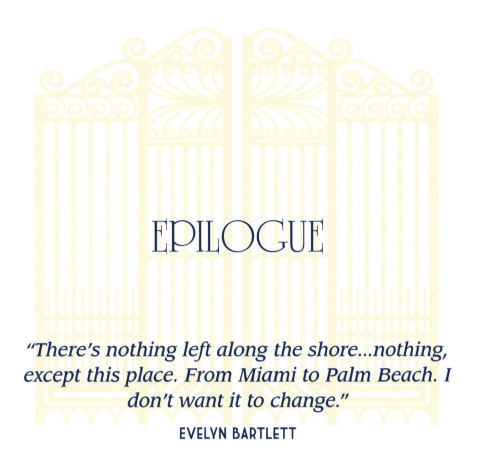

"There's nothing left along the shore...nothing, except this place. From Miami to Palm Beach. I don't want it to change."

EVELYN BARTLETT

All the Bartletts and Birches who created here are now gone. Frederic's son, Clay, also an accomplished painter, died in 1955, just two years after his father. Evelyn Bartlett's only daughter, Evie, who created ceramics for her mother, predeceased her by 27 years, in 1970, at age 52. But Frederic's granddaughter, Elisabeth Sturges, generously helped make this commemorative edition possible, and other Bartlett and Fortune descendants provide ongoing support to the museum.

Beyond these first families of Bonnet House, many others today nurture its continuing creative spirit. Artists train, create, and display their work here. Orchid enthusiasts learn how to grow and care for their plants. Elementary and high school students – many at risk – come here to study art, cultural history, and the environment. Young musicians gain valuable experience performing under the stars for winter audiences. In addition, a dedicated corps of three hundred volunteers is daily inspired to share this special place with our visitors, many of whom call or write to tell us how their visit re-energized their love of art, history, or the environment – or their own personal creativity. Perhaps the most creative force of all comes from the couples who wed here almost every weekend during the winter season.

(above) Music lovers enjoy concerts under the stars on balmy winter evenings.

(middle and right) An annual juried art competition, *Impressions of Florida*, raises funds for Bonnet House and provides a festive evening for those who attend its opening night.

On weekends throughout the year, couples exchange wedding vows in the lush tropical setting.

Guests at Bonnet House may tour the lush grounds as well as the unusual house.

An eclectic estate that is the most significant and enduring achievement of a creative team of families, Bonnet House truly is a place that inspires learning and creativity:

Bonnet House Museum & Gardens reflects the broad sweep of American history through both the indigenous peoples who lived here and the European explorers who followed them.

It reflects a unique glimpse of cultural history through the minority staff who worked and raised their families here in an environment of love and respect from their employers.

It reflects the history of American art, through artists who produced visual art, poetry, and music within the cultural trends of their times.

It reflects American architectural history through a design that blends vernacular style with Caribbean and even Middle-Eastern influences, perhaps subtly and whimsically mimicking a renowned architect who had mentored its creator.

It reflects how the environment can be adapted to private use and integrated with non-native elements while still retaining its intrinsic nature.

Bonnet House Museum & Gardens is a historic house museum that today uniquely contributes – and far into the future will continue to contribute – to the advancement of a wide variety of learning and creativity for all who pass through its gates.

BARTLETT/BIRCH/FORTUNE FAMILY TREE

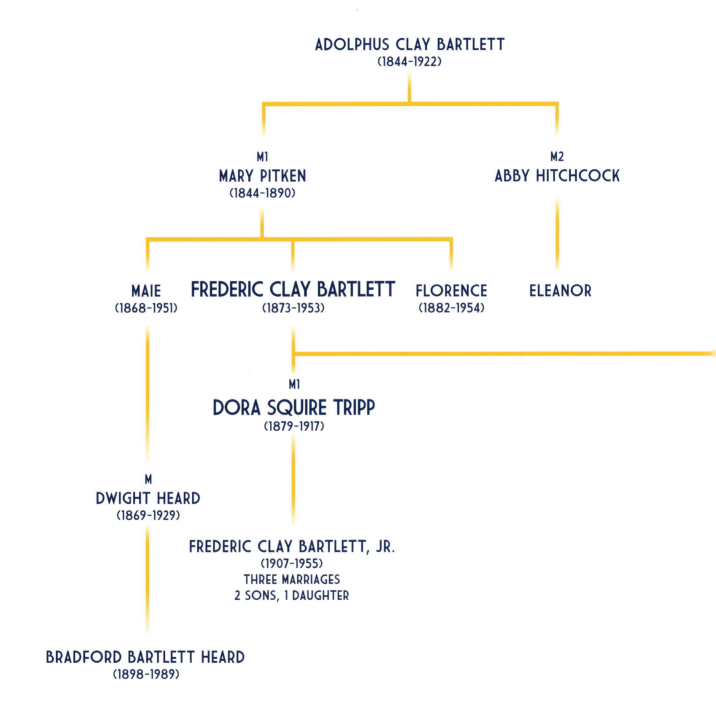

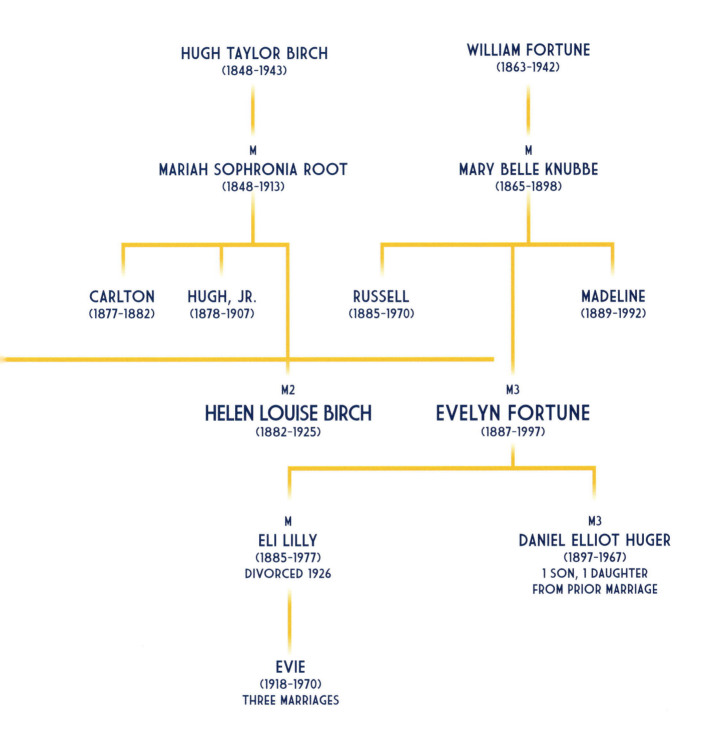

CREDITS

Bonnet House extends its sincere thanks to all those who made gifts in support of the publication of this book:

Lynn Arimoto
Blair Bartlett
Clay Bartlett, Jr.
Clay Bartlett, Sr.
Colleen Bartlett
Elise Bartlett
Karen and Richard Beard
Virginia Bécart
Albert Beveridge III
Bonnet House Alliance
Ron Bourgeault
Heather Brock and Edwin Parkinson III
E. Paige Drummond Brody
Bobbie Burke
Sandy Casteel
Barbara Castell
Martha and Mike Chapman
Becky Clarke
Greg Coble
Elizabeth Conner and Timothy L. Hernandez
Arthur Crispino and Anthony Timiraos
Donation in Honor of William Dennis
Mr. and Mrs. William L. Elder
Dianne Ennis
Monica Estevez
Jane Fortune
Penny and Jock Fortune
Joan and Peter Fortune
William L. Fortune, Jr. and Joseph D. Blakley
Ray George
Stuart Gilbert
Katherine Guida and Vincent Botta
James Horan
Kirk Imhof and David Bolus
Scott LaMont
Barbara and Tom Keith

Geri Manning and Buck Schottland
Connie and Mike McNerney
Bruce Montgomery
Harry K. Moon, M.D.
Dev Motwani
Northern Trust Bank, Chicago
Elizabeth Parker
Sherry Parker
Susan M. Parker
Diana and Ralph Rau
Lois and John Schmatz
Patrick Shavloske and Mark Gerberding
Pat and Dennis Smith
William R. Stanton
Scott Strawbridge
Elisabeth Bartlett Sturges
Donation in Memory of Jessie Kent Sturges
Peter Sturges
Judith Taylor
Susan Taylor
Stephanie Toothaker and Peter Kemp
Christopher Webber
Alexandra Wentworth and
    George Stephanopoulos
Ben Wentworth
Eric Bartlett Wentworth
Jan Wentworth
John Wentworth
Tom Wentworth
Mary Wilcox
R. Marshall Witten
Sissy and Angus Yates
Anonymous

Special thanks goes to the author, J. Kent Planck, an active docent at Bonnet House, who contributed countless hours of time in researching and producing *Bonnet House: A Legacy of Artistry and Elegance.*

Thanks also goes to Wingate Payne, an active docent as well, for her assistance in editing the text.

PHOTO AND IMAGE CREDITS

Courtesy of Antiochiana, Antioch College, page 46 (top).

© Bonnet House Archives, pages 2, 6 (top), 7, 10 (top), 33, 34, 38 (top and right), 39 (top), 45, 46 (bottom), 47, 48, 49, 50 (top), 51, 52, 53, 58 (right), 59 (center), 61, 62, 66, 68.

Clay Bartlett, *Island Theater*, 1944, watercolor on paper, 24 x 28 in., 2006.BH.657, Bonnet House Museum & Gardens. Photography © Bonnet House Museum & Gardens, page 31.

Frederic Clay Bartlett, *Blue Rafters*, c. 1916, oil on canvas, 28 x 30¼ in., Friends of American Art Collection, 1919.107, The Art Institute of Chicago. Photography © The Art Institute of Chicago, p. 58 (center).

Frederic Clay Bartlett, *Bonnet House from the Tower*, c. 1935, oil on canvas, 28¼ x 31¼ in., 1985.B.002, Bonnet House Museum & Gardens. Photography © Bonnet House Museum & Gardens, page 44.

Frederic Clay Bartlett, *Evelyn at Whitehall*, c. 1931, oil on canvas, 59¼ x 59½ in., 1998.FB.197, Bonnet House Museum & Gardens. Photograph © Bonnet House Museum & Gardens, page 19 (top).

Frederic Clay Bartlett, Nymphenglade panel, (reproduction by Amy Smetanick), c. 1939, oil on wood, 29 x 30 in., 1990.FB.017, Bonnet House Museum & Gardens. Photography © J. Christopher Gernert, page 40 (bottom).

Frederic Clay Bartlett, Nymphenglade panel, (reproduction by Amy Smetanick), c. 1939, oil on wood, 29 x 30 in., 1990.FB.026, Bonnet House Museum & Gardens. Photography © J. Christopher Gernert, page 40 (top).

Frederic Clay Bartlett, student drawing, 1893, charcoal on paper, 19 x 24 in., 1990.FB.106, Bonnet House Museum & Gardens. Photography © J. Christopher Gernert, page 19 (bottom left).

Frederic Clay Bartlett, student drawing, 1894, charcoal on paper, 17½ x 23 in., 1985.B.046, Bonnet House Museum & Gardens. Photography © J. Christopher Gernert, page 19 (bottom left).

Frederic Clay Bartlett and Evelyn Fortune Bartlett, logia ceiling, c. 1931-1954, oil on wood, 127 x 168 in., 1990.FB.002, Bonnet House Museum & Gardens. Photography © J. Christopher Gernert, page 25.

Evelyn Fortune Bartlett, *Catherine Eddy Beveridge*, c. 1935, oil on canvas, private collection. Photograph © Bonnet House Museum & Gardens, page 41 (top).

Evelyn Fortune Bartlett, *Yellow Coat*, c. 1935, oil on canvas, 34 x 37 in., 1986.EB.030, Bonnet House Museum & Gardens. Photograph © Bonnet House Museum & Gardens, page 41 (bottom).

© Tony Branco, pages 1, 8, 11 (top), 15 (bottom), 28 (bottom), 29 (bottom right), 30, 31 (top), 59 (right), 65 (bottom), 67 (bottom), 69, 71, 72, 79.

© Steven Brooke, pages 55, 56, 57, 59 (left), 67 (top).

Paul Cezanne, *The Basket of Apples*, c. 1893, oil on canvas, 25 7/16 x 31½ in., Helen Birch Bartlett Memorial Collection, 1926.252, The Art Institute of Chicago. Photography © The Art Institute of Chicago, page 35.

© Sandy Dolan (Bonnet House Fine Artist), page 11 (bottom), 15 (top), 18 (top), 28 (top), 32, 36, 37 (bottom), 78.

© Sandy Dolan (Bonnet House Fine Artist), *Whispering Behind Mama's Back*, page 13 (bottom).

© Don DuBroff, page 65 (top).

© David W. Fischer, *Fall Color at the Cascades*, page 73.

© Annie Garrick (Bonnet House Fine Artist), pages 6 (bottom), 10 (bottom), 12, 13 (top).

© J. Christopher Gernert, J. Christopher Photography (Bonnet House Fine Artist), pages 14 (bottom), 16, 20, 21, 22, 23, 24 (bottom), 26, 29 (bottom left), 37 (top), 42, 43, 70, 74.

Steve Hall © Hedrich Blessing, pages 60, 64.

Bill Hedrich © Hedrich Blessing, page 63.

© Michael Kitei, pages 18 (bottom), 30 (bottom).

© Daniel Routhier (Bonnet House Fine Artist), *Bonnet House Slough*, page 4.

Georges Seurat, *A Sunday on La Grande Jatte—1884*, 1884-86, oil on canvas, 81¾ x 121¼ in., Helen Birch Bartlett Memorial Collection, 1926.224, The Art Institute of Chicago. Photography © The Art Institute of Chicago, page 35.

Pablo Picasso, *The Old Guitarist*, late 1903-early 1904, oil on panel, 48⅜ x 32½ in., Helen Birch Bartlett Memorial Collection, 1926.253, The Art Institute of Chicago. Photography © The Art Institute of Chicago, page 35.

© John D. Pearce, page 24 (top).

© Smith Aerial Photos, page 50 (bottom).

© Richard Viola, pages 14 (top), 29 top, 38 (left), 39 (bottom).

© Clay Wieland, pages 76, 77.

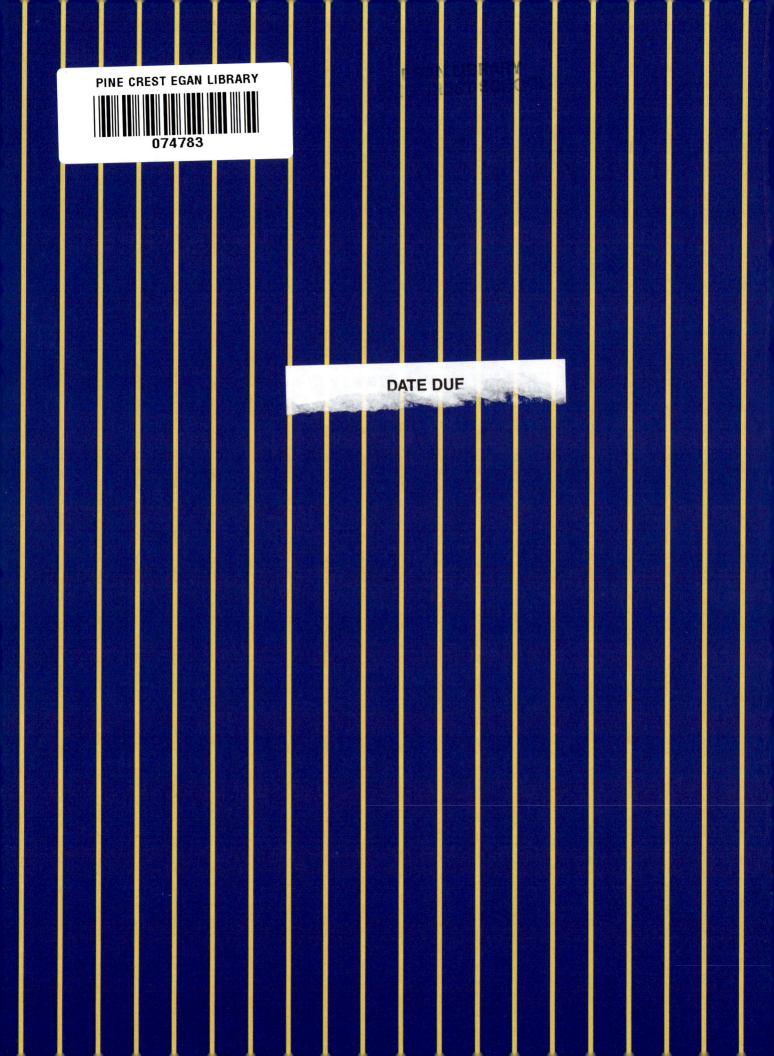